Good
Tidings
of
Great Joy

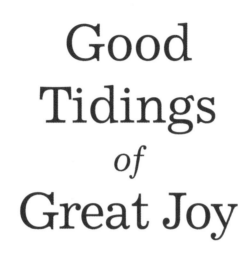

Good Tidings

of

Great Joy

The Biblical Story of Christmas
in One Seamless Narrative

FEATURING OLD AND NEW TESTAMENT PASSAGES
FROM THE NEW KING JAMES VERSION™

THOMAS NELSON
Since 1798

Good Tidings of Great Joy: The Biblical Story of
Christmas in One Seamless Narrative
© 2018 by Thomas Nelson, a division of HarperCollins
Christian Publishing, Inc.

 The Holy Bible, New King James Version®
Copyright © 1982 by Thomas Nelson.

Senior Editor: John Greco
Cover Design: Halie Cotton
Interior Design and Layout: Holly Wittenberg
Interior and cover art © Shutterstock and © iStockphoto

Printed in China

20 21 22 23 24 25 /GRI/ 17 16 15 14 13 12 11 10 9 8 7 6 5 4 3 2 1

FOREWORD

With holiday songs on the radio, decorations in the stores, and twinkle lights on the houses, the holiday season is upon us once again. But even with reminders of Christmas everywhere, many people don't really know what the celebration is all about. Now, they may know it has something to do with Jesus' birth, but beyond that, they can tell you little about that incredible night in Bethlehem over two thousand years ago.

What happened in that small village on the outskirts of the Roman Empire changed the world, and we believe that knowing the story—the whole story— can change your world as well. As with any important message, it's best to go directly to the source. In

this case, we would do well to go back to the Bible, to let God's Spirit, who inspired the very words of Scripture, tell us about the first Christmas.

The book you hold in your hands contains the story of Christmas from Scripture. No words have been changed, but the pieces of the narrative, taken from several books of the Bible, have been woven together to form one seamless tale, the greatest true story ever told. In these pages, you'll meet the virgin Mary and her righteous fiancé, Joseph. You'll see shepherds leaving their flocks to seek out the newborn king and wise men from the East falling down to worship Him. And you'll hear the angels and prophets proclaim that the Child who was placed in the manger is the long-awaited Messiah, the Savior of the world.

Maybe this is your first time reading about the Son of God who loved you enough to trade the glories of heaven for the humility of the manger. Or maybe you think you've heard all there is to know. Either way, our prayer is that this book will help you read the story of Christmas with fresh eyes. And we hope you'll share it with the ones you love, making the biblical story of Jesus' birth a part of your annual Christmas traditions. You may even find yourself pulling this little book off the shelf in March or July, if only to get another taste of Christmas—the true story of the Son of God and His great love for you.

—The Editorial Team at Thomas Nelson Bibles

PROLOGUE

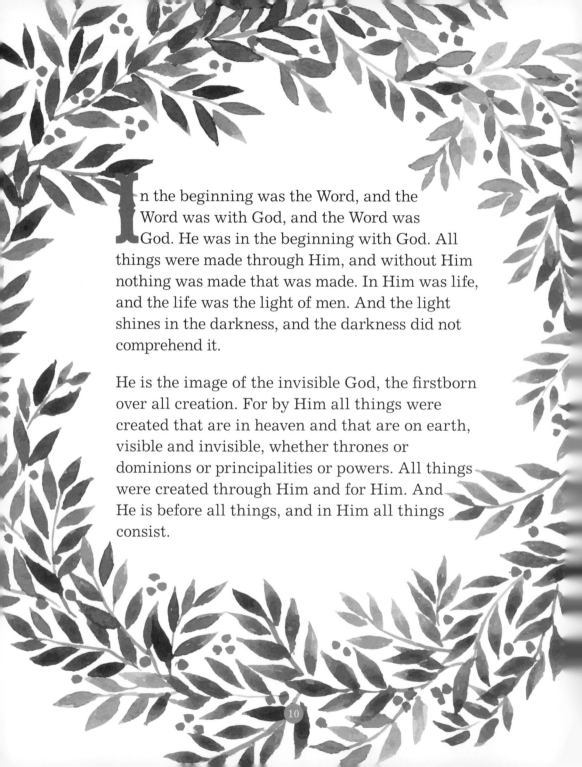

In the beginning was the Word, and the Word was with God, and the Word was God. He was in the beginning with God. All things were made through Him, and without Him nothing was made that was made. In Him was life, and the life was the light of men. And the light shines in the darkness, and the darkness did not comprehend it.

He is the image of the invisible God, the firstborn over all creation. For by Him all things were created that are in heaven and that are on earth, visible and invisible, whether thrones or dominions or principalities or powers. All things were created through Him and for Him. And He is before all things, and in Him all things consist.

"Behold, I send My
   messenger,
And he will prepare the
   way before Me. . . .
Behold, He is coming,"
Says the LORD of hosts.

There was a man sent from
God, whose name was John.
This man came for a witness,
to bear witness of the Light, that all
through him might believe. He was not that
Light, but was sent to bear witness of that
Light. That was the true Light which gives light
to every man coming into the world.

ONE

There was in the days of Herod, the king of Judea, a certain priest named Zacharias, of the division of Abijah. His wife was of the daughters of Aaron, and her name was Elizabeth. And they were both righteous before God, walking in all the commandments and ordinances of the Lord blameless. But they had no child, because Elizabeth was barren, and they were both well advanced in years.

So it was, that while he was serving as priest before God in the order of his division, according to the custom of the priesthood, his lot fell to burn incense when he went into the temple of the Lord. And the whole multitude of the people was praying outside at the hour of incense. Then an angel of the Lord appeared to him, standing on the right side of the altar of incense. And when Zacharias saw him, he was troubled, and fear fell upon him.

But the angel said to him, "Do not be afraid, Zacharias, for your prayer is heard; and your wife Elizabeth will bear you a son, and you shall call his name John. And you will have joy and gladness, and many will rejoice at his birth. For he will be great in the sight of the Lord, and shall drink neither wine nor strong drink. He will also be filled with the Holy Spirit, even from his mother's womb. And he will turn many of the children of Israel to the Lord their God. He will also go before Him in the spirit and power of Elijah, 'to turn the hearts of the fathers to the children,' and the disobedient to the wisdom of the just, to make ready a people prepared for the Lord."

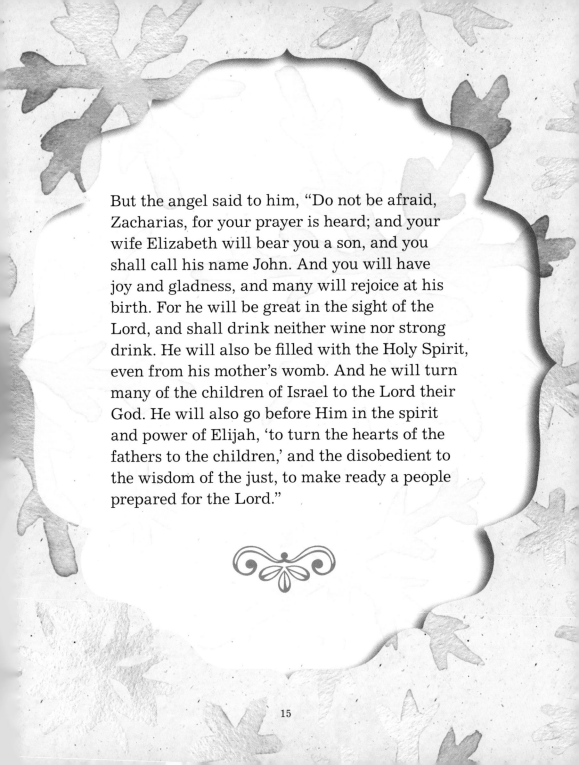

The voice of one crying in the wilderness:
"Prepare the way of the Lord;
Make straight in the desert
A highway for our God.
Every valley shall be exalted
And every mountain and hill brought low;
The crooked places shall be made straight
And the rough places smooth;
The glory of the Lord shall be revealed,
And all flesh shall see it together;
For the mouth of the Lord has spoken."

And Zacharias said to the angel, "How shall I know this? For I am an old man, and my wife is well advanced in years."

And the angel answered and said to him, "I am Gabriel, who stands in the presence of God, and was sent to speak to you and bring you these glad tidings. But behold, you will be mute and not able to speak until the day these things take place, because you did not believe my words which will be fulfilled in their own time."

And the people waited for Zacharias, and marveled that he lingered so long in the temple. But when he came out, he could not speak to them; and they perceived that he had seen a vision in the temple, for he beckoned to them and remained speechless.

So it was, as soon as the days of his service were completed, that he departed to his own house. Now after those days his wife Elizabeth conceived; and she hid herself five months, saying, "Thus the Lord has dealt with me, in the days when He looked on me, to take away my reproach among people."

TWO

✦•──•─•─•─•─•─•─•─•──•✦

Now in the sixth month the angel Gabriel was sent by God to a city of Galilee named Nazareth, to a virgin betrothed to a man whose name was Joseph, of the house of David. The virgin's name was Mary. And having come in, the angel said to her, "Rejoice, highly favored one, the Lord is with you; blessed are you among women!"

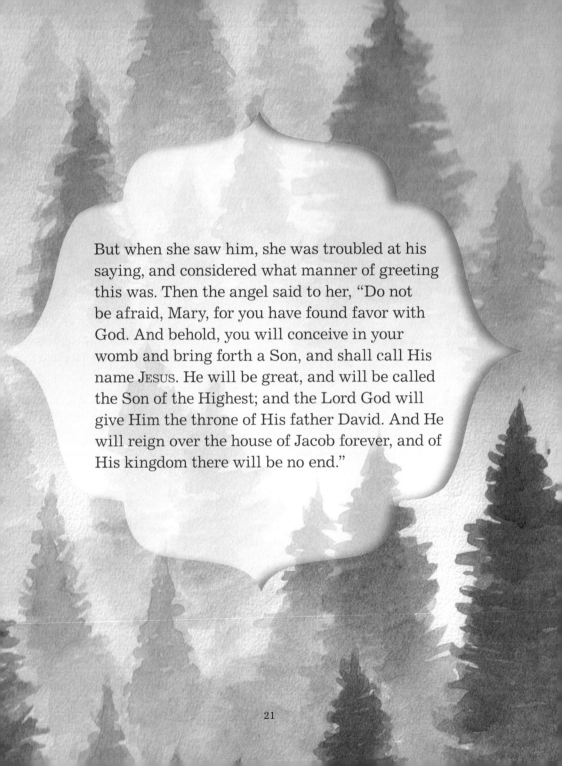

But when she saw him, she was troubled at his saying, and considered what manner of greeting this was. Then the angel said to her, "Do not be afraid, Mary, for you have found favor with God. And behold, you will conceive in your womb and bring forth a Son, and shall call His name Jesus. He will be great, and will be called the Son of the Highest; and the Lord God will give Him the throne of His father David. And He will reign over the house of Jacob forever, and of His kingdom there will be no end."

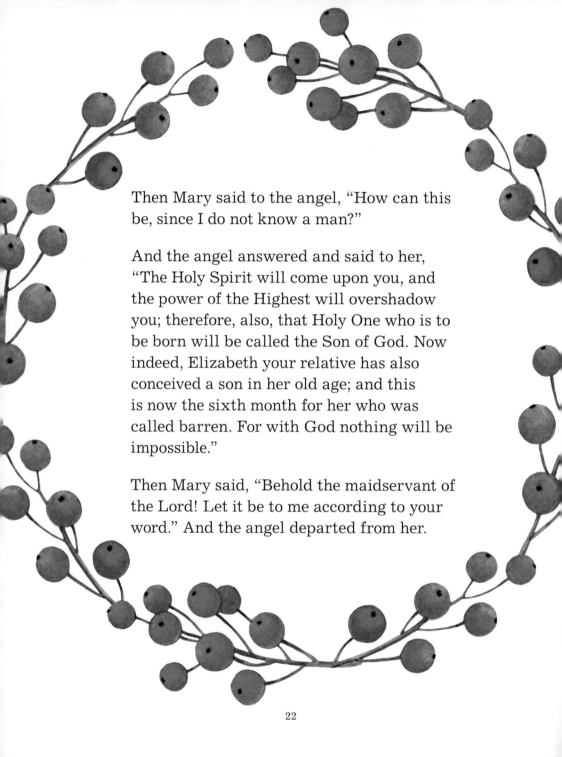

Then Mary said to the angel, "How can this be, since I do not know a man?"

And the angel answered and said to her, "The Holy Spirit will come upon you, and the power of the Highest will overshadow you; therefore, also, that Holy One who is to be born will be called the Son of God. Now indeed, Elizabeth your relative has also conceived a son in her old age; and this is now the sixth month for her who was called barren. For with God nothing will be impossible."

Then Mary said, "Behold the maidservant of the Lord! Let it be to me according to your word." And the angel departed from her.

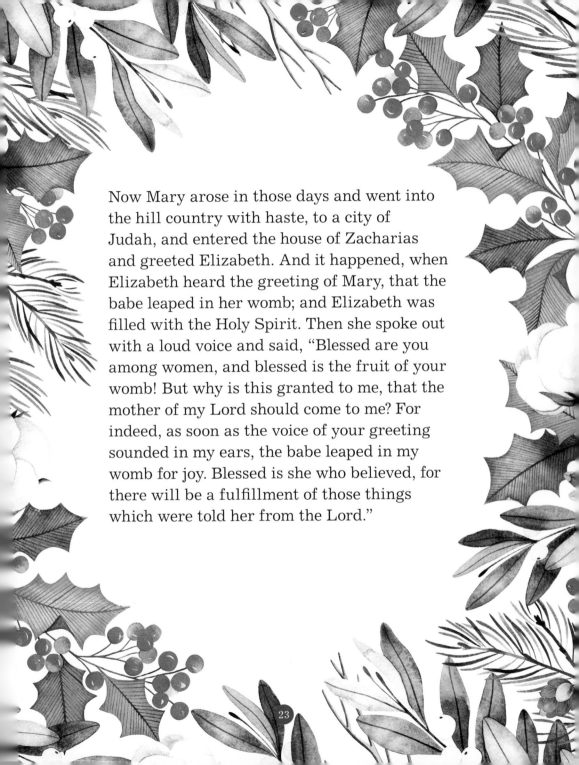

Now Mary arose in those days and went into the hill country with haste, to a city of Judah, and entered the house of Zacharias and greeted Elizabeth. And it happened, when Elizabeth heard the greeting of Mary, that the babe leaped in her womb; and Elizabeth was filled with the Holy Spirit. Then she spoke out with a loud voice and said, "Blessed are you among women, and blessed is the fruit of your womb! But why is this granted to me, that the mother of my Lord should come to me? For indeed, as soon as the voice of your greeting sounded in my ears, the babe leaped in my womb for joy. Blessed is she who believed, for there will be a fulfillment of those things which were told her from the Lord."

And Mary said:

"My soul magnifies the Lord,
And my spirit has rejoiced in God my Savior.
For He has regarded the lowly state of His maidservant;
For behold, henceforth all generations will call me
    blessed.
For He who is mighty has done great things for me,
And holy is His name.
And His mercy is on those who fear Him
From generation to generation.
He has shown strength with His arm;
He has scattered the proud in the imagination of their
    hearts.
He has put down the mighty from their thrones,
And exalted the lowly.
He has filled the hungry with good
    things,
And the rich He has sent away empty.
He has helped His servant Israel,
In remembrance of His mercy,
As He spoke to our fathers,
To Abraham and to his seed forever."

And Mary remained with
her about three months,
and returned to
her house.

THREE

• • • • • • • • •

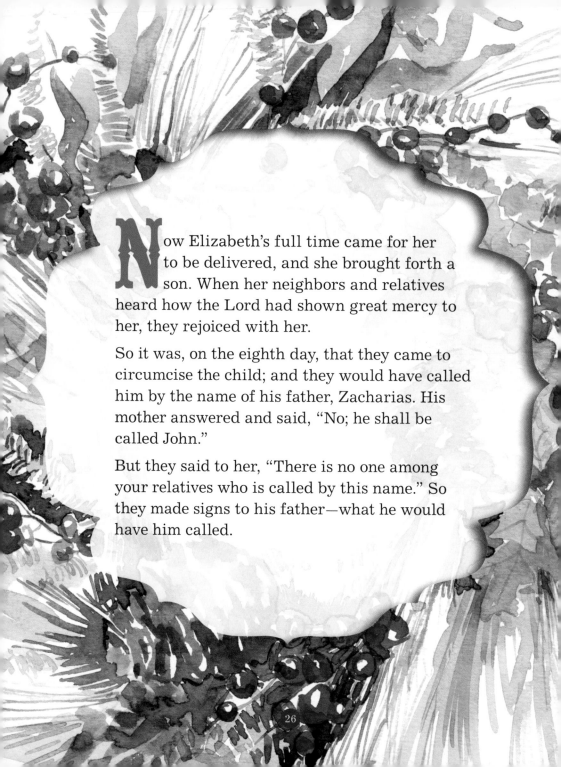

Now Elizabeth's full time came for her to be delivered, and she brought forth a son. When her neighbors and relatives heard how the Lord had shown great mercy to her, they rejoiced with her.

So it was, on the eighth day, that they came to circumcise the child; and they would have called him by the name of his father, Zacharias. His mother answered and said, "No; he shall be called John."

But they said to her, "There is no one among your relatives who is called by this name." So they made signs to his father—what he would have him called.

And he asked for a writing tablet, and wrote, saying, "His name is John." So they all marveled. Immediately his mouth was opened and his tongue loosed, and he spoke, praising God. Then fear came on all who dwelt around them; and all these sayings were discussed throughout all the hill country of Judea. And all those who heard them kept them in their hearts, saying, "What kind of child will this be?" And the hand of the Lord was with him.

Now his father Zacharias was filled with the Holy
Spirit, and prophesied, saying:

"Blessed is the Lord God of Israel,
For He has visited and redeemed His people,
And has raised up a horn of salvation for us
In the house of His servant David,
As He spoke by the mouth of His holy prophets,
Who have been since the world began,
That we should be saved from our enemies
And from the hand of all who hate us,
To perform the mercy promised to our fathers
And to remember His holy covenant,
The oath which He swore to our father Abraham:
To grant us that we,
Being delivered from the hand of our enemies,
Might serve Him without fear,
In holiness and righteousness before Him
    all the days of our life.

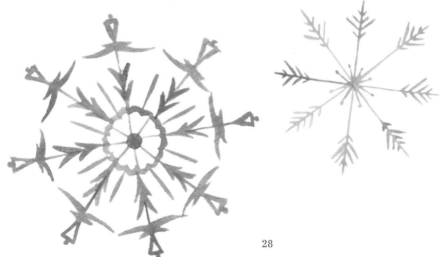

"And you, child, will be called the prophet of the
    Highest;
For you will go before the face of the Lord to
    prepare His ways,
To give knowledge of salvation to His people
By the remission of their sins,
Through the tender mercy of our God,
With which the Dayspring from on high has
    visited us;
To give light to those who sit in darkness and
    the shadow of death,
To guide our feet into the way of peace."

So the child grew and became strong in spirit,
and was in the deserts till the day of his
manifestation to Israel.

FOUR

Now the birth of Jesus Christ was as follows: After His mother Mary was betrothed to Joseph, before they came together, she was found with child of the Holy Spirit. Then Joseph her husband, being a just man, and not wanting to make her a public example, was minded to put her away secretly. But while he thought about these things, behold, an angel of the Lord appeared to him in a dream, saying, "Joseph, son of David, do not be afraid to take to you Mary your wife, for that which is conceived in her is of the Holy Spirit. And she will bring forth a Son, and you shall call His name JESUS, for He will save His people from their sins."

So all this was done that it might be fulfilled which was spoken by the Lord through the prophet, saying: "Behold, the virgin shall be with child, and bear a Son, and they shall call His name Immanuel," which is translated, "God with us."

"The LORD your God in your midst,
The Mighty One, will save;
He will rejoice over you with gladness,
He will quiet you with His love,
He will rejoice over you with singing."

Then Joseph, being aroused from sleep, did as the angel of the Lord commanded him and took to him his wife, and did not know her till she had brought forth her firstborn Son.

And it came to pass
in those days that a
decree went out
from Caesar Augustus
that all the world should be
registered. This census first
took place while Quirinius was
governing Syria. So all went to be
registered, everyone to his own city.

Joseph also went up from Galilee, out
of the city of Nazareth, into Judea,
to the city of David, which is called
Bethlehem, because he was of the house
and lineage of David, to be registered
with Mary, his betrothed wife, who was
with child. So it was, that while they
were there, the days were completed for
her to be delivered. And she brought forth
her firstborn Son, and wrapped Him in
swaddling cloths, and laid Him in a manger,
because there was no room for them in the inn.

"But you, Bethlehem Ephrathah,
Though you are little among the
        thousands of Judah,
Yet out of you shall come forth to Me
The One to be Ruler in Israel,
Whose goings forth are from of old,
From everlasting."

FIVE

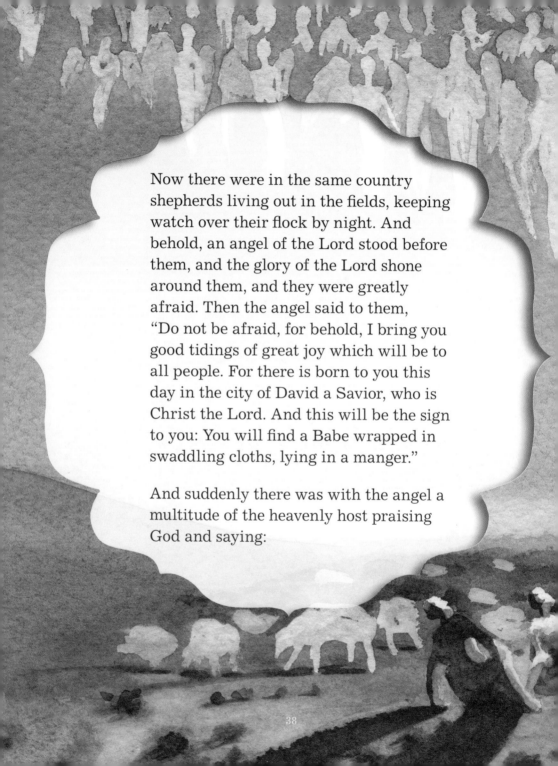

Now there were in the same country shepherds living out in the fields, keeping watch over their flock by night. And behold, an angel of the Lord stood before them, and the glory of the Lord shone around them, and they were greatly afraid. Then the angel said to them, "Do not be afraid, for behold, I bring you good tidings of great joy which will be to all people. For there is born to you this day in the city of David a Savior, who is Christ the Lord. And this will be the sign to you: You will find a Babe wrapped in swaddling cloths, lying in a manger."

And suddenly there was with the angel a multitude of the heavenly host praising God and saying:

"Glory to God in the highest,
And on earth peace, goodwill
toward men!"

Oh, sing to the LORD a new song!
For He has done marvelous things;
His right hand and His holy arm have gained
   Him the victory.
The LORD has made known His salvation;
His righteousness He has revealed in the sight of
   the nations.
He has remembered His mercy and His
   faithfulness to the house of Israel;
All the ends of the earth have seen the salvation
   of our God.

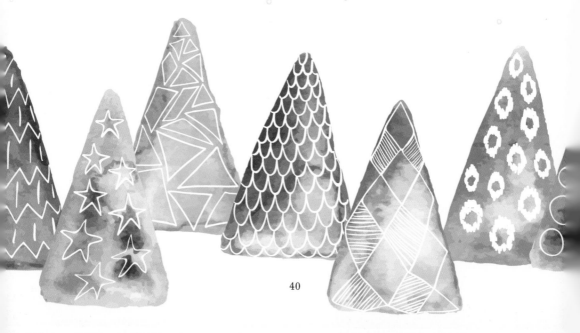

40

Shout joyfully to the LORD, all the earth;
Break forth in song, rejoice, and sing praises.
Sing to the LORD with the harp,
With the harp and the sound of a psalm,
With trumpets and the sound of a horn;
Shout joyfully before the LORD, the King.
Let the sea roar, and all its fullness,
The world and those who dwell in it;
Let the rivers clap their hands;
Let the hills be joyful together before the LORD,
For He is coming to judge the earth.
With righteousness He shall judge the world,
And the peoples with equity.

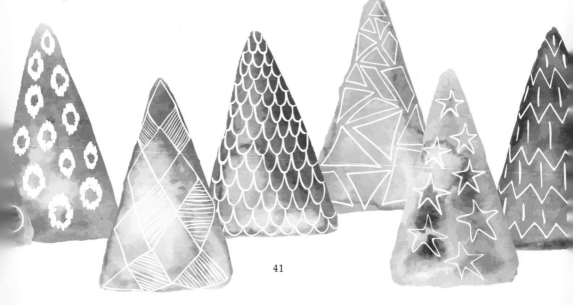

So it was, when the angels had gone away
from them into heaven, that the shepherds
said to one another, "Let us now go to
Bethlehem and see this thing that has come
to pass, which the Lord has made known to
us." And they came with haste and found
Mary and Joseph, and the Babe lying in a
manger. Now when they had seen Him, they
made widely known the saying which was
told them concerning this Child. And all those
who heard it marveled at those things which
were told them by the shepherds. But Mary
kept all these things and pondered them in her
heart. Then the shepherds returned, glorifying
and praising God for all the things that they
had heard and seen, as it was told them.

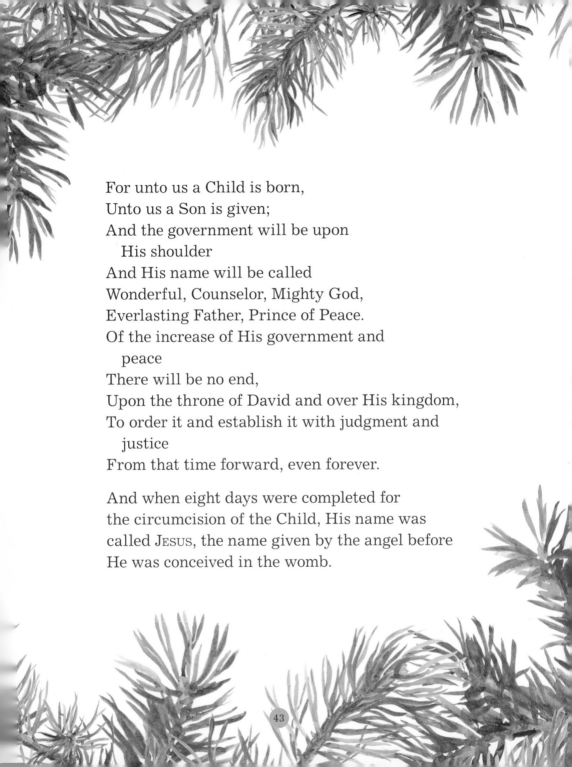

For unto us a Child is born,
Unto us a Son is given;
And the government will be upon
   His shoulder
And His name will be called
Wonderful, Counselor, Mighty God,
Everlasting Father, Prince of Peace.
Of the increase of His government and
   peace
There will be no end,
Upon the throne of David and over His kingdom,
To order it and establish it with judgment and
   justice
From that time forward, even forever.

And when eight days were completed for
the circumcision of the Child, His name was
called Jesus, the name given by the angel before
He was conceived in the womb.

SIX

ow when the days of her purification according to the law of Moses were completed, they brought Him to Jerusalem to present Him to the Lord (as it is written in the law of the Lord, "Every male who opens the womb shall be called holy to the LORD"), and to offer a sacrifice according to what is said in the law of the Lord, "A pair of turtledoves or two young pigeons."

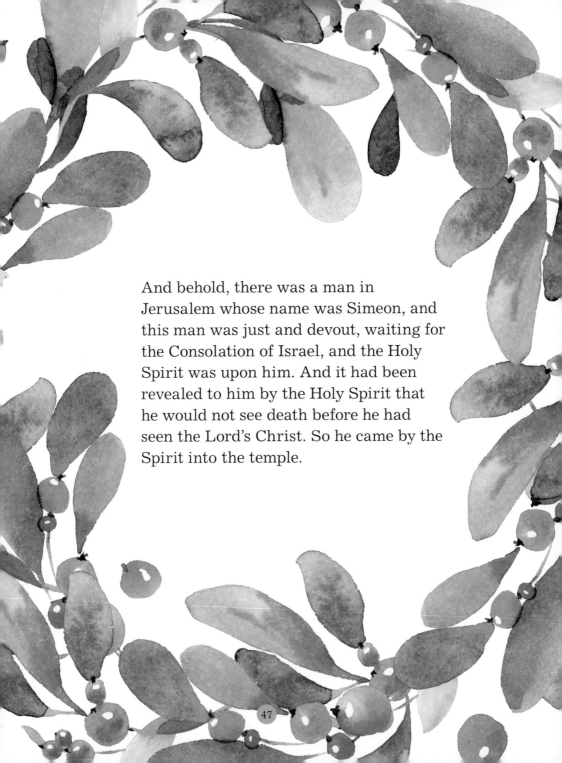

And behold, there was a man in
Jerusalem whose name was Simeon, and
this man was just and devout, waiting for
the Consolation of Israel, and the Holy
Spirit was upon him. And it had been
revealed to him by the Holy Spirit that
he would not see death before he had
seen the Lord's Christ. So he came by the
Spirit into the temple.

And when the parents brought in the Child
Jesus, to do for Him according to the custom of
the law, he took Him up in his arms and blessed
God and said:

"Lord, now You are letting Your servant depart
    in peace,
According to Your word;
For my eyes have seen Your salvation
Which You have prepared before the face of all
    peoples,
A light to bring revelation to the Gentiles,
And the glory of Your people Israel."

By the way of the sea, beyond the Jordan,
In Galilee of the Gentiles.
The people who walked in darkness
Have seen a great light;
Those who dwelt in the land of the shadow of
    death,
Upon them a light has shined.

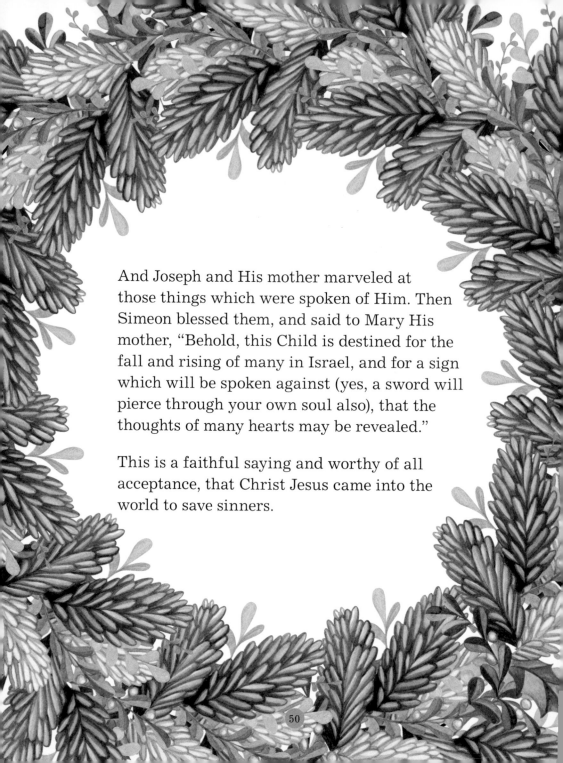

And Joseph and His mother marveled at those things which were spoken of Him. Then Simeon blessed them, and said to Mary His mother, "Behold, this Child is destined for the fall and rising of many in Israel, and for a sign which will be spoken against (yes, a sword will pierce through your own soul also), that the thoughts of many hearts may be revealed."

This is a faithful saying and worthy of all acceptance, that Christ Jesus came into the world to save sinners.

Now there was one, Anna, a prophetess, the daughter of Phanuel, of the tribe of Asher. She was of a great age, and had lived with a husband seven years from her virginity; and this woman was a widow of about eighty-four years, who did not depart from the temple, but served God with fastings and prayers night and day. And coming in that instant she gave thanks to the Lord, and spoke of Him to all those who looked for redemption in Jerusalem.

SEVEN

Now after Jesus was born in Bethlehem of Judea in the days of Herod the king, behold, wise men from the East came to Jerusalem, saying, "Where is He who has been born King of the Jews? For we have seen His star in the East and have come to worship Him."

"A Star shall come out of Jacob;
A Scepter shall rise out of Israel."

When Herod the king heard this, he was troubled, and all Jerusalem with him. And when he had gathered all the chief priests and scribes of the people together, he inquired of them where the Christ was to be born.

So they said to him, "In Bethlehem of Judea, for thus it is written by the prophet:

'But you, Bethlehem, in the land of Judah,
Are not the least among the rulers of Judah;
For out of you shall come a Ruler
Who will shepherd My people Israel.'"

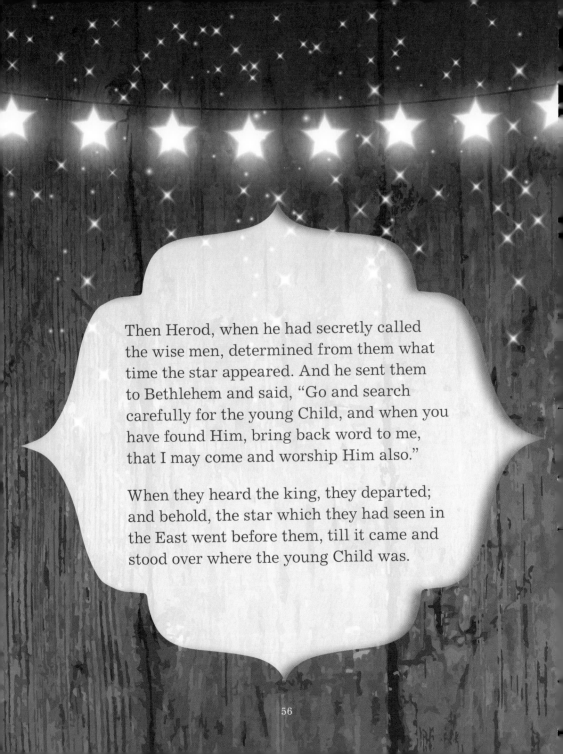

Then Herod, when he had secretly called the wise men, determined from them what time the star appeared. And he sent them to Bethlehem and said, "Go and search carefully for the young Child, and when you have found Him, bring back word to me, that I may come and worship Him also."

When they heard the king, they departed; and behold, the star which they had seen in the East went before them, till it came and stood over where the young Child was.

When they saw the star, they rejoiced with exceedingly great joy. And when they had come into the house, they saw the young Child with Mary His mother, and fell down and worshiped Him. And when they had opened their treasures, they presented gifts to Him: gold, frankincense, and myrrh.

Then, being divinely warned in a dream that they should not return to Herod, they departed for their own country another way.

EIGHT

·•·•·•·•·•·•·•·

ow when they had departed, behold, an angel of the Lord appeared to Joseph in a dream, saying, "Arise, take the young Child and His mother, flee to Egypt, and stay there until I bring you word; for Herod will seek the young Child to destroy Him."

When he arose, he took the young Child and His mother by night and departed for Egypt, and was there until the death of Herod, that it might be fulfilled which was spoken by the Lord through the prophet, saying, "Out of Egypt I called My Son."

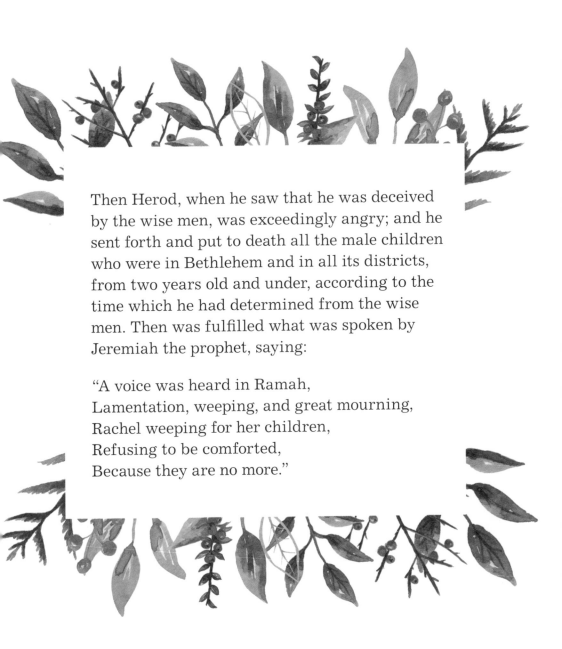

Then Herod, when he saw that he was deceived by the wise men, was exceedingly angry; and he sent forth and put to death all the male children who were in Bethlehem and in all its districts, from two years old and under, according to the time which he had determined from the wise men. Then was fulfilled what was spoken by Jeremiah the prophet, saying:

"A voice was heard in Ramah,
Lamentation, weeping, and great mourning,
Rachel weeping for her children,
Refusing to be comforted,
Because they are no more."

Now when Herod was dead, behold, an angel of the Lord appeared in a dream to Joseph in Egypt, saying, "Arise, take the young Child and His mother, and go to the land of Israel, for those who sought the young Child's life are dead." Then he arose, took the young Child and His mother, and came into the land of Israel.

But when he heard that Archelaus was reigning over Judea instead of his father Herod, he was afraid to go there. And being warned by God in a dream, he turned aside into the region of Galilee. And he came and dwelt in a city called Nazareth, that it might be fulfilled which was spoken by the prophets, "He shall be called a Nazarene."

For He shall grow up before Him as a tender
   plant,
And as a root out of dry ground.
He has no form or comeliness;
And when we see Him,
There is no beauty that we should desire Him.

And Jesus increased in wisdom and stature, and in favor with God and men.

NINE

Now Jesus Himself began His ministry at about thirty years of age.

In those days John the Baptist came preaching in the wilderness of Judea.

"I indeed baptize you with water unto repentance, but He who is coming after me is mightier than I, whose sandals I am not worthy to carry."

"Behold! The Lamb of God who takes away the sin of the world!"

From that time Jesus began to preach and to say, "Repent, for the kingdom of heaven is at hand."

"I am the bread of *life*. He who comes to Me shall never hunger, and he who believes in Me shall never thirst.

"I am the light of the world. He who follows Me shall not walk in darkness, but have the light of *life*."

"I am the resurrection and the *life*. He who believes in Me, though he may die, he shall live."

"I have come that they may have *life*, and that they may have it more abundantly."

"For God so loved the world that He gave His only begotten Son, that whoever believes in Him should not perish but have everlasting *life*."

"For even the Son of Man did not come to be served, but to serve, and to give His *life* a ransom for many."

Let this mind be in you which was also in Christ Jesus, who, being in the form of God, did not consider it robbery to be equal with God, but made Himself of no reputation, taking the form of a bondservant, and coming in the likeness of men. And being found in appearance as a man, He humbled Himself and became obedient to the point of death, even the death of the cross. Therefore God also has highly exalted Him and given Him the name which is above every name, that at the name of Jesus every knee should bow, of those in heaven, and of those on earth, and of those under the earth, and that every tongue should confess that Jesus Christ is Lord, to the glory of God the Father.

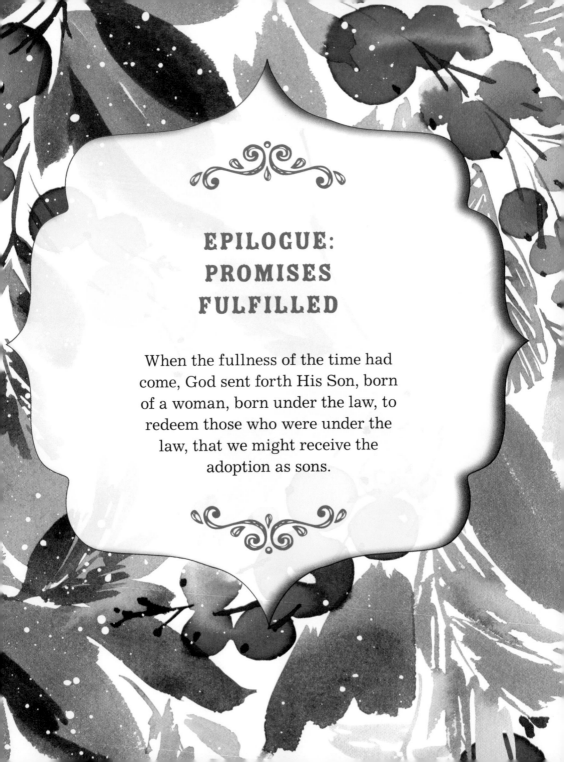

EPILOGUE: PROMISES FULFILLED

When the fullness of the time had come, God sent forth His Son, born of a woman, born under the law, to redeem those who were under the law, that we might receive the adoption as sons.

Now the LORD had said to Abram:

"Get out of your country,
From your family
And from your father's house,
To a land that I will show you.
I will make you a great nation;
I will bless you
And make your name great;
And you shall be a blessing.
I will bless those who bless you,
And I will curse him who curses you;
And in you all the families of the
earth shall be blessed."

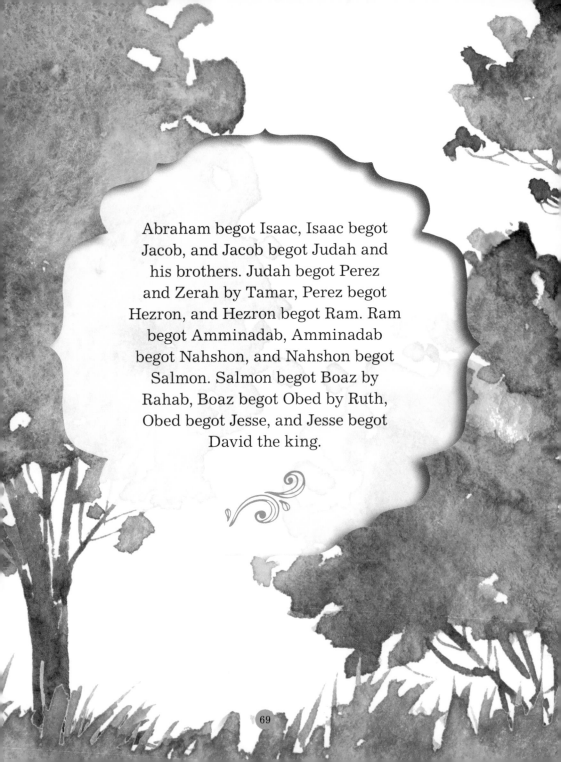

Abraham begot Isaac, Isaac begot Jacob, and Jacob begot Judah and his brothers. Judah begot Perez and Zerah by Tamar, Perez begot Hezron, and Hezron begot Ram. Ram begot Amminadab, Amminadab begot Nahshon, and Nahshon begot Salmon. Salmon begot Boaz by Rahab, Boaz begot Obed by Ruth, Obed begot Jesse, and Jesse begot David the king.

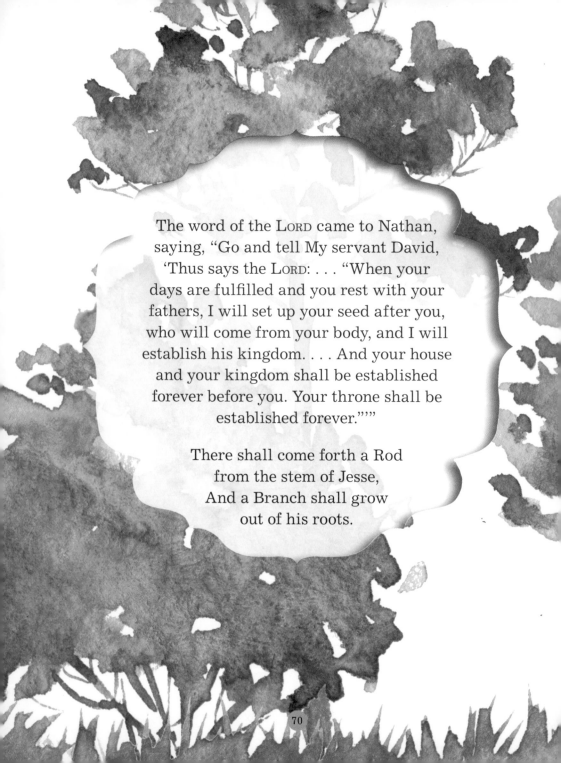

The word of the LORD came to Nathan, saying, "Go and tell My servant David, 'Thus says the LORD: . . . "When your days are fulfilled and you rest with your fathers, I will set up your seed after you, who will come from your body, and I will establish his kingdom. . . . And your house and your kingdom shall be established forever before you. Your throne shall be established forever."'"

There shall come forth a Rod
from the stem of Jesse,
And a Branch shall grow
out of his roots.

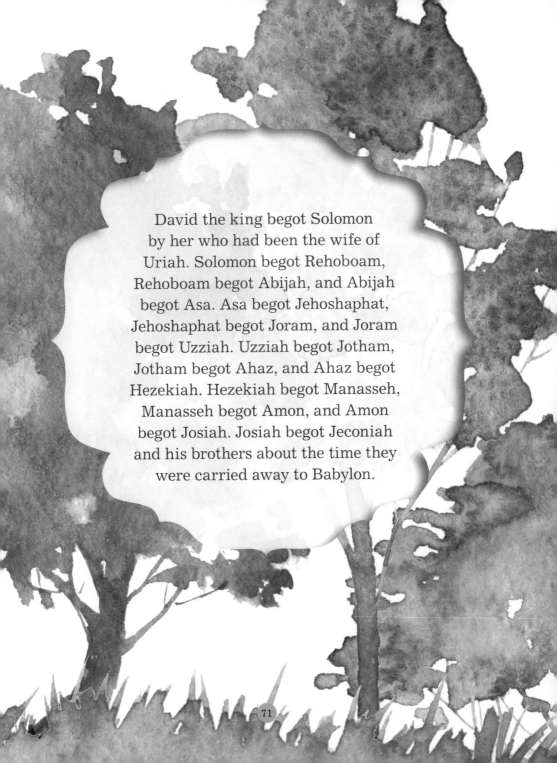

David the king begot Solomon
by her who had been the wife of
Uriah. Solomon begot Rehoboam,
Rehoboam begot Abijah, and Abijah
begot Asa. Asa begot Jehoshaphat,
Jehoshaphat begot Joram, and Joram
begot Uzziah. Uzziah begot Jotham,
Jotham begot Ahaz, and Ahaz begot
Hezekiah. Hezekiah begot Manasseh,
Manasseh begot Amon, and Amon
begot Josiah. Josiah begot Jeconiah
and his brothers about the time they
were carried away to Babylon.

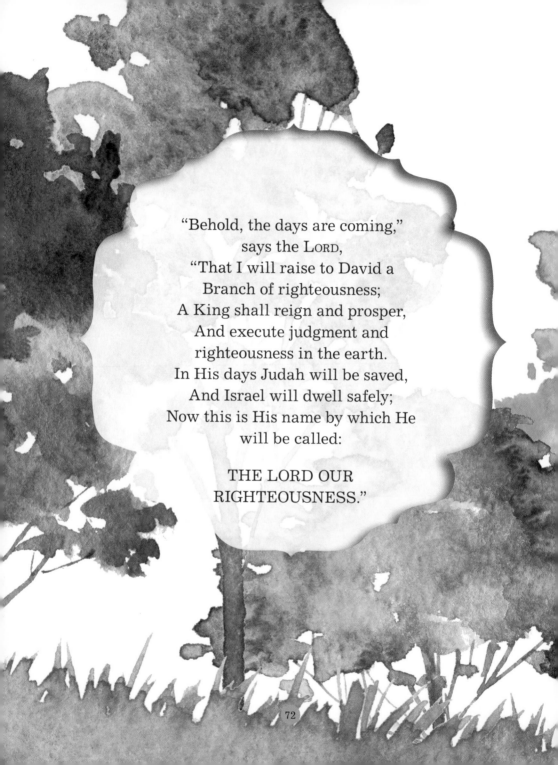

"Behold, the days are coming,"
says the Lord,
"That I will raise to David a
Branch of righteousness;
A King shall reign and prosper,
And execute judgment and
righteousness in the earth.
In His days Judah will be saved,
And Israel will dwell safely;
Now this is His name by which He
will be called:

THE LORD OUR
RIGHTEOUSNESS."

And after they were brought
to Babylon, Jeconiah begot
Shealtiel, and Shealtiel begot
Zerubbabel. Zerubbabel begot Abiud,
Abiud begot Eliakim, and Eliakim
begot Azor. Azor begot Zadok, Zadok
begot Achim, and Achim begot
Eliud. Eliud begot Eleazar, Eleazar
begot Matthan, and Matthan begot
Jacob. And Jacob begot Joseph the
husband of Mary, of whom was born
Jesus who is called Christ.

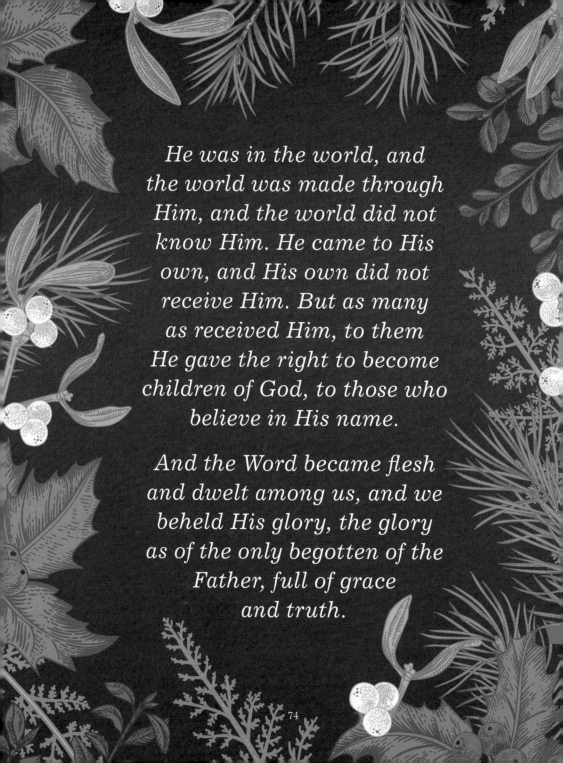

He was in the world, and the world was made through Him, and the world did not know Him. He came to His own, and His own did not receive Him. But as many as received Him, to them He gave the right to become children of God, to those who believe in His name.

And the Word became flesh and dwelt among us, and we beheld His glory, the glory as of the only begotten of the Father, full of grace and truth.

BONUS SECTION: FAVORITE CHRISTMAS HYMNS

Hark! The Herald Angels Sing

Charles Wesley   Felix Mendelssohn

1. Hark! the her - ald an - gels sing,   "Glo - ry to the new - born King;
2. Christ, by high - est heav'n a - dored,   Christ, the ev - er - last - ing Lord;
3. Hail the heav'n born Prince of Peace!   Hail the Sun of Righ-teous-ness!

Peace on earth and mer - cy mild,   God and sin - ners rec - on - ciled."
Late in time be - hold Him come,   Off - spring of a vir - gin's womb.
Light and life to all He brings,   Ris'n with heal - ing in His wings.

Joy - ful, all ye na - tions, rise,   Join the tri - umph of the skies;
Veiled in flesh the God - head see,   Hail, th'in - car - nate De - i - ty!
Mild He lays His glo - ry by,   Born that man no more may die;

With an - gel - ic hosts pro - claim,   "Christ is born in Beth - le - hem."
Pleased as man with men to dwell,   Je - sus our Em - man - u - el.
Born to raise the sons of earth,   Born to give them sec - ond birth.

Hark! The herald angels sing,
"Glory to the newborn King;
Peace on earth and mercy mild,
God and sinners reconciled."
Joyful all ye nations rise,
Join the triumph of the skies;
With angelic hosts proclaim,
"Christ is born in Bethlehem."

Christ, by highest heav'n adored,
Christ the everlasting Lord;
Late in time behold Him come,
Offspring of a virgin's womb.
Veiled in flesh the Godhead see,
Hail, th'incarnate Deity!
Pleased as man with men to dwell,
Jesus our Emmanuel.

Hail the heav'n born Prince of Peace!
Hail the Sun of Righteousness!
Light and life to all He brings,
Ris'n with healing in His wings.
Mild He lays His glory by,
Born that man no more may die;
Born to raise the sons of earth,
Born to give them second birth.

O come all ye faithful,
Joyful and triumphant,
O come ye, O come ye to Bethlehem.
Come and behold Him,
Born the King of angels.
O come let us adore Him,
O come let us adore Him,
O come let us adore Him,
Christ the Lord.

Sing choirs of angels,
Sing in exultation,
O sing all ye bright Hosts of heav'n above.
Glory to God,
All glory in the highest,
O come let us adore Him,
O come let us adore Him,
O come let us adore Him,
Christ the Lord.

Yea, Lord we greet Thee,
Born this happy morning;
Jesus to Thee be all glory giv'n.
Word of the Father
Now in flesh appearing.
O come let us adore Him,
O come let us adore Him,
O come let us adore Him,
Christ the Lord.

O Come, All Ye Faithful

ascribed to John Francis Wade

translated by Frederick Oakeley

John Francis Wade

1. O come all ye faith - ful, Joy - ful and tri - um - phant, O
2. Sing choirs of an - gels, Sing in ex - ul - ta - tion, O
3. Yea, Lord, we greet Thee, Born this hap - py morn - ing;

come ye, O come ye to Beth - le - hem. Come and be -
sing all ye bright Hosts of heav'n a - bove. Glo - ry to
Je - sus to Thee be all glo - ry giv'n. Word of the

hold Him, Born the King of an - gels.
God, All glo - ry in the high - est. O come let us a - dore Him, O
Fa - ther Now in flesh ap - pear - ing.

Refrain

come let us a - dore Him, O come let us a - dore Him, Christ the Lord.

Angels, from the Realms of Glory

James Montgomery

Henry T. Smart

1. An - gels from the realms of glo - ry, Wing your flight o'er
2. Shep - herds in the fields a - bi - ding, Watch - ing o'er your
3. Sag - es, leave your con - tem - pla - tions, Bright - er vi - sions
4. Saints, be - fore the al - tar bend - ing, Watch - ing long in
5. All cre - a - tion, join in prais - ing, God, the Fath - er,

all the earth; Ye who sang cre - a - tion's sto - ry,
flocks by night; God with man is now re - sid - ing,
beam a - far; Seek the great De - sire of na - tions,
hope and fear; Sud - den - ly the Lord, de - scend - ing,
Spir - it, Son; Ev - er - more your voic - es rais - ing,

Now pro - claim Mes - si - ah's birth.
Yon - der shines the in - fant Light.
Ye have seen His na - tal star.
In His tem - ple shall ap - pear.
To th'et - er - nal Three in One.

Come and wor - ship, come and wor - ship; Wor - ship Christ, the new - born King!

Angels from the realms of glory,
Wing your flight o'er all the earth;
Ye who sang creation's story,
Now proclaim Messiah's birth.
Come and worship, come and worship;
Worship Christ, the newborn King!

Shepherds in the fields abiding,
Watching o'er your flocks by night;
God with man is now residing,
Yonder shines the infant Light.
Come and worship, come and worship;
Worship Christ, the newborn King!

Sages, leave your contemplations,
Brighter visions beam afar;
Seek the great Desire of nations,
Ye have seen His natal star.
Come and worship, come and worship;
Worship Christ, the newborn King!

Saints, before the altar bending,
Watching long in hope and fear;
Suddenly the Lord, descending,
In His temple shall appear.
Come and worship, come and worship;
Worship Christ, the newborn King!

All creation, join in praising,
God, the Father, Spirit, Son;
Evermore your voices raising,
To th'eternal Three in One.
Come and worship, come and worship;
Worship Christ, the newborn King!

Silent night, holy night,
All is calm, all is bright.
Round yon virgin mother and child;
Holy infant, so tender and mild,
Sleep in heavenly peace;
Sleep in heavenly peace.

Silent night, holy night,
Shepherds quake at the sight.
Glories stream from heaven afar,
Heavenly hosts sing "Alleluia.
Christ the Savior is born;
Christ the Savior is born."

Silent night, holy night,
Wondrous star, lend thy light.
With the angels, let us sing,
Alleluia to our King.
Christ the Savior is born;
Christ the Savior is born.

Silent night, holy night,
Son of God, love's pure light.
Radiant beams from Thy holy face,
With the dawn of redeeming grace.
Jesus, Lord, at Thy birth;
Jesus, Lord, at Thy birth.

Silent Night

Joseph Mohr

Franz Gruber

1. Si - lent night, ho - ly night, All is calm,
2. Si - lent night, ho - ly night, Shep - herds quake
3. Si - lent night, ho - ly night, Won - drous star,
4. Si - lent night, ho - ly night, Son of God,

all is bright. Round yon vir - gin moth - er and child;
at the sight. Glo - ries stream from heav - en a - far,
lend thy light. With the an - gels, let us sing,
love's pure light. Ra - diant beams from Thy ho - ly face,

Ho - ly in - fant, so ten - der and mild, Sleep in heav - en - ly
Heaven - ly hosts sing "Al - le - lu - ia. Christ the Sa - vior is
Al - le - lu - ia to our King. Christ the Sa - vior is
With the dawn of re - deem - ing grace. Je - sus, Lord, at Thy

peace; Sleep in heav - en - ly peace.
born; Christ the Sav - ior is born."
born; Christ the Sa - vior is born.
birth; Je - sus, Lord, at Thy birth.

It Came upon the Midnight Clear

Edmund H. Sears

Richard Storrs Willis

1. It came up-on the mid-night clear, That glo-rious song of old;
2. Still thro' the clo-ven skies they come, With peace-ful wings un-furled;
3. For lo, the days are has-tening on, By proph-et bards fore-told;

From an-gels bend-ing near the earth To touch their harps of gold.
And still their heaven-ly mu-sic floats, O'er all the wear-y world.
When with the ev-er-cir-cling years, Comes round the age of gold.

"Peace on the earth good will to men, From heaven's all gra-cious King!"
A-bove its sad and low-ly plains, They bend on hov-ering wing;
When peace shall o-ver all the earth, Its an-cient splen-dors fling;

The world in sol-emn still-ness lay To hear the an-gels sing.
And ev-er o'er its Ba-bel sounds The bless-ed an-gels sing.
And the whole world give back the song Which now the an-gels sing.

It came upon the midnight clear,
That glorious song of old;
From angels bending near the earth
To touch their harps of gold.
"Peace on the earth good will to men,
From heaven's all gracious King!"
The world in solemn stillness lay
To hear the angels sing.

Still thro' the cloven skies they come,
With peaceful wings unfurled;
And still their heavenly music floats,
O'er all the weary world.
Above its sad and lowly plains,
They bend on hovering wing;
And ever o'er its Babel sounds
The blessed angels sing.

For lo, the days are hastening on,
By prophet bards foretold;
When with the ever circling years,
Comes round the age of gold.
When peace shall over all the earth,
Its ancient splendors fling;
And the whole world give back the song
Which now the angels sing.

85

O little town of Bethlehem,
How still we see thee lie;
Above thy deep and dreamless sleep,
The silent stars go by.
Yet in thy dark streets shineth
The everlasting Light;
The hopes and fears of all the years,
Are met in thee tonight.

For Christ is born of Mary
And gathered all above;
While mortals sleep the angels keep
Their watch of wondering love.
O, morning stars together
Proclaim the holy birth;
And praises sing to God the King
And peace to men on earth.

How silently, how silently,
The wondrous gift is giv'n;
So God imparts to human hearts,
The blessings of His heaven.
No ear may hear His coming,
But in this world of sin;
Where meek souls will Receive Him still,
The dear Christ enters in.

O, holy child of Bethlehem,
Descend to us we pray;
Cast out our sin and enter in,
Be born in us today.
We hear the Christmas angels,
The great glad tidings tell;
O, come to us abide with us,
Our Lord Emmanuel.

O Little Town of Bethlehem

Phillips Brooks

Lewis H. Redner

1. O little town of Beth-le-hem, How still we see thee lie;
2. For Christ is born of Ma - ry And gath-ered all a - bove;
3. How si - lent-ly, how si - lent-ly, The won-drous gift is giv'n;
4. O, ho - ly child of Beth-le-hem, De - scend to us we pray;

A - bove thy deep and dream-less sleep, The si - lent stars go by.
While mor-tals sleep the an - gels keep Their watch of won-dering love.
So God im-parts to hu - man hearts, The bless-ings of His heaven.
Cast out our sin and en - ter in, Be born in us to - day.

Yet in thy dark streets shin - eth The ev - er - last - ing Light;
O, morn - ing stars to - geth - er Pro - claim the ho - ly birth;
No ear may hear His com - ing, But in this world of sin;
We hear the Christ-mas an - gels, The great glad tid - ings tell;

The hopes and fears of all the years, Are met in thee to-night.
And prais - es sing to God the King And peace to men on earth.
Where meek souls will Re - ceive Him still, The dear Christ en - ters in.
O, come to us a - bide with us, Our Lord, Em - man - u - el.

87

YEAR	WHO READ THE STORY

YEAR

WHO READ THE STORY

_____   _____

_____   _____

_____   _____

_____   _____

_____   _____

_____   _____

_____   _____

_____   _____

_____   _____

_____   _____

_____   _____

_____   _____

_____   _____

_____   _____

YEAR

WHO READ THE STORY

_____ _____

_____ _____

_____ _____

_____ _____

_____ _____

_____ _____

_____ _____

_____ _____

_____ _____

_____ _____

_____ _____

_____ _____

_____ _____

_____ _____

_____ _____

YEAR

WHO READ THE STORY

FAVORITE CHRISTMAS MEMORIES

_____

_____

_____

_____

_____

_____

_____

_____

_____

_____

_____

_____

_____

_____

_____

FAVORITE CHRISTMAS MEMORIES

_____

_____

_____

_____

_____

_____

_____

_____

_____

_____

_____

_____

_____

_____

_____

_____

_____

SCRIPTURE REFERENCES